TRIANGLE ★ HISTORIES
★ ★ ★ ★ ★ ★ ★ ★ ★
THE REVOLUTIONARY WAR

CHARLES CORNWALLIS

Lewis K. Parker

BLACKBIRCH®
PRESS

THOMSON
───── ✦ ─────
GALE

San Diego • Detroit • New York • San Francisco • Cleveland
New Haven, Conn. • Waterville, Maine • London • Munich

For more information, contact
The Gale Group, Inc.
27500 Drake Rd.
Farmington Hills, MI 48331-3535
Or you can visit our Internet site at http://www.gale.com

LIBRARY OF CONGRESS CATALOGING-IN-PUBLICATION DATA

Parker, Lewis K.
  Charles Cornwallis / by Lewis K. Parker.
    p. cm. — (Triangle history of the American Revolution. Revolutionary War leaders)
  Includes index.
   ISBN 1-56711-608-6 (lib. bdg. : alk. paper)
   1. Cornwallis, Charles Cornwallis, Marquis, 1738-1805-Juvenile literature. 2. Generals—Great Britain—Biography—Juvenile literature. 3. United States—History—Revolution, 1775-1783-British forces—Juvenile literature. 4. United States—History—Revolution, 1775-1783—Campaigns—Juvenile literature. [1. Cornwallis, Charles Cornwallis, Marquis, 1738-1805. 2. Generals. 3. United States—History—Revolution, 1775-1783.] I. Title. II. Series.
   DA67.1.C77 P37 2003
   973.3'41'092—dc21   2002005336

Printed in China
10 9 8 7 6 5 4 3 2 1

CONTENTS

PREFACE: THE AMERICAN REVOLUTION

Today, more than two centuries after the final shots were fired, the American Revolution remains an inspiring story not only to Americans, but also to people around the world. For many citizens, the well-known battles that occurred between 1775 and 1781—such as Lexington, Trenton, Yorktown, and others—represent the essence of the Revolution. In truth, however, the formation of the United States involved much more than the battles of the Revolutionary War. The creation of our nation occurred over several decades, beginning in 1763, at the end of the French and Indian War, and continuing until 1790, when the last of the original 13 colonies ratified the Constitution.

More than 200 years later, it may be difficult to fully appreciate the courage and determination of the people who fought for, and founded, our nation. The decision to declare independence was not made easily—and it was not unanimous. Breaking away from England—the ancestral land of most colonists—was a bold and difficult move. In addition to the emotional hardship of revolt, colonists faced the greatest military and economic power in the world at the time.

The first step on the path to the Revolution was essentially a dispute over money. By 1763, England's treasury had been drained in order to pay for the French and Indian War. British lawmakers, as well as England's new ruler, King George III, felt that the colonies should help to pay for the war's expense and for the cost of housing the British troops who remained in the colonies. Thus began a series of oppressive British tax acts and other laws that angered the colonists and eventually provoked full-scale violence.

King George III

The Stamp Act of 1765 was followed by the Townshend
Acts in 1767. Gradually, colonists were forced to pay
taxes on dozens of everyday goods from playing cards to
paint to tea. At the same time, the colonists had no say in
the passage of these acts. The more colonists complained
that "taxation without representation is tyranny," the
more British lawmakers claimed the right to make laws

for the colonists "in all cases whatsoever." Soldiers and tax collectors were sent to the colonies to enforce the new laws. In addition, the colonists were forbidden to trade with any country but England.

Each act of Parliament pushed the colonies closer to unifying in opposition to English laws. Boycotts of British goods inspired protests and violence against tax collectors. Merchants who continued to trade with the Crown risked attacks by their colonial neighbors. The rising violence soon led to riots against British troops stationed in the colonies and the organized destruction of British goods. Tossing tea into Boston Harbor was just one destructive act. That event, the Boston Tea Party, led England to pass the so-called Intolerable Acts of 1774. The port of Boston was closed, more British troops were sent to the colonies, and many more legal rights for colonists were suspended.

Finally, there was no turning back. Early on an April morning in 1775, at Lexington Green in Massachusetts, the first shots of the American Revolution were fired. Even after the first battle, the idea of a war against England seemed unimaginable to all but a few radicals. Many colonists held out hope that a compromise could be reached. Except for the Battle of Bunker Hill and some minor battles at sea, the war ceased for much of 1775. During this time, delegates to the Continental Congress struggled to reach a consensus about the next step.

During those uncertain months, the Revolution was fought, not on a military battlefield, but on the battlefield of public opinion. Ardent rebels—especially Samuel Adams and Thomas Paine—worked tirelessly to keep the spirit of revolution alive. They stoked the fires of revolt by writing letters and pamphlets, speaking at public gatherings, organizing boycotts, and devising other forms of protest. It was their brave efforts that kept others focused on liberty and freedom until July 4, 1776. On that day, Thomas Jefferson's Declaration of Independence left no doubt about the intentions of the colonies. As John Adams wrote afterward, the "revolution began in hearts and minds not on the battlefield."

As unifying as Jefferson's words were, the United States did not become a nation the moment the Declaration of Independence claimed the right of all people to "life, liberty, and the pursuit of happiness." Before, during, and after the war, Americans who spoke of their "country" still generally meant whatever colony was their home. Some colonies even had their own navies during the war, and a few sent their own representatives to Europe to seek aid for their colony alone while delegates from the Continental Congress were doing the same job for the whole United States. Real national unity did not begin to take hold until the inauguration of George Washington in 1789, and did not fully bloom until the dawn of the 19th century.

The story of the American Revolution has been told for more than two centuries and may well be told for centuries to come. It is a tribute to the men and women who came together during this unique era that, to this day, people the world over find inspiration in the story of the Revolution. In the words of the Declaration of Independence, these great Americans risked "their lives, their fortunes, and their sacred honor" for freedom.

The Minuteman statue stands in Concord, Massachusetts.

Introduction:
"Tired of Marching"

By 1781, General Lord Charles Cornwallis had been commander of the British forces in the southern colonies for nearly a year. Although he had been successful throughout the war, his command gave him little pleasure.

A respected officer and military strategist, he had actually resigned from the army in 1778 to tend to his dying wife. Devastated by her death in 1779, Cornwallis had requested that King George III restore his commission. A soldier's life was all he knew, and it was the only way he believed he could escape the sadness of a loved one's death.

In 1780, after he took part in the conquest of Charleston, South Carolina, Cornwallis had been given command of British southern forces by General Henry Clinton upon Clinton's return to New York City. Throughout much of 1780, Cornwallis's crack troops, brutal cavalry, and Loyalist militia had destroyed American forces in South Carolina.

For Cornwallis, however, the year 1781 began badly. In January, his force was defeated at the Battle of Cowpens, South Carolina, by an American force led by General Nathanael Greene and militia under General Daniel Morgan.

For the next several months, Greene led Cornwallis on a chase across North Carolina.

As the British marched across South Carolina, they were harassed by American militia and by Patriot forces.

Greene's forces used harassing raids that destroyed the spirit of the British regulars, who could not pin down the elusive Patriots. Cornwallis, a man once called "the best soldier in the British army," was constantly outfoxed by Greene, his ragged regulars, and the buckskin-clad militia sharpshooters.

In April 1781, a frustrated Cornwallis wrote to Clinton that he was "quite tired of marching about the country." To win the war, he wrote, "we must...bring our whole force into Virginia."

Cornwallis soon did exactly that—he sent his men into Virginia and won several small battles against overmatched American forces there. Unfortunately for the British, however, that decision ultimately proved disastrous to their efforts to win the war.

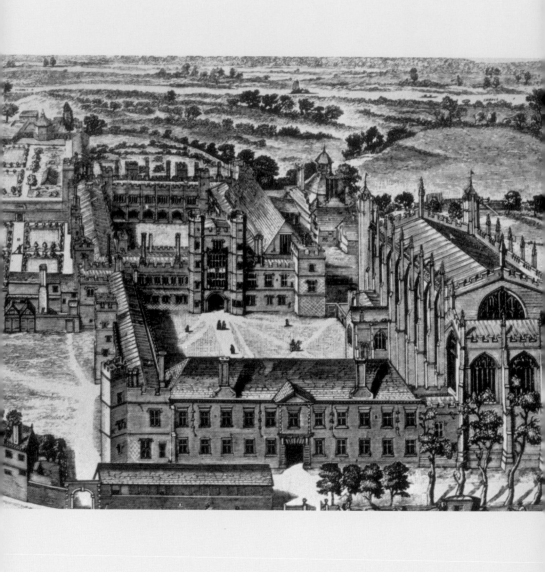

Chapter 1

BECOMING
A SOLDIER

Charles Cornwallis was born in London, England, on December 31, 1738. He was the sixth child and eldest son of Earl Charles Cornwallis and Elizabeth, daughter of Lord Townshend. Cornwallis's family was not wealthy, but family members could trace their roots back to the 14th century. One member of his family had been the sheriff of London. For generations, his family had been landowners and members of England's nobility, the ruling class that held seats in one chamber of the British Parliament, the House of Lords.

OPPOSITE: As a young man, Cornwallis attended Eton, a private boarding school popular with England's wealthy nobles.

In the 17th century, King Charles II had made Frederick Cornwallis, Charles's great-grandfather, a baron as a reward for faithful service. Cornwallis's father, also named Charles, was the first Earl Cornwallis. An uncle was the archbishop of Canterbury.

Cornwallis was raised in comfort at his family's estate, Brome Hall, in Suffolk, which is located in eastern England. As a child, he was called Lord Brome and was raised like all young members of British society of the time. He learned to ride a horse soon after he could walk. He often rode in fox hunts. He also learned to shoot a gun, mainly to hunt pheasants in the forests near his home.

As an adolescent, Cornwallis attended Eton, a private boarding school where many future statesmen and military men of England received their education. Eton's teachers believed it was their duty to mold the country's future leaders. Students were expected to become tough enough to handle any hardship or challenge. At that time, teachers at Eton—and in most English private schools—beat students who misbehaved or failed in their lessons.

Sports at Eton went beyond mere competition— students were encouraged to use fists, elbows, knees, or whatever was needed to win games. As a student, Cornwallis received a scar for life when a hockey puck struck a hard blow to his eye.

Many of Cornwallis's classmates at Eton went on to universities such as Oxford and Cambridge for further education. Cornwallis took a different path. He wanted to distinguish himself in the military.

In December 1756, when he was almost eighteen years old, he accepted a commission in the First, or Grenadier, Guards. His father bought Charles the rank of ensign, which was the way most army officers began their careers. Cornwallis could have continued to buy commissions and rise to the rank of general without any real experience in battle. He was eager, however, to earn glory in a war.

At that time, there was no academy in England to train infantry and cavalry officers. In order to learn military skills, Cornwallis had to leave England. In 1757, he attended a military academy in Turin, Italy, which was considered one of the best in Europe.

By that time, England was at war with France over control of the territory in the Ohio River Valley and Canada in North America. Both countries had formed alliances with European powers, and some battles took place in western Europe. The war, known as the French and Indian War in the American colonies, was called the Seven Years' War in Europe.

Throughout 1758, Cornwallis saw action in Europe. He performed well and was promoted quickly. In August 1759, he rose to captain in the 85th Foot Guards. In May 1761, he was promoted to commander of his own regiment, the 12th Foot Guards, with the rank of lieutenant colonel.

In 1762, Cornwallis learned that his father had died. When he went home to England, he had inherited the title of Earl Cornwallis. That November, he replaced his father in Parliament and took a seat in the House of Lords.

During the years that he fought in Europe, he had grown from a boy into a man. Before his 24th birthday, he had become an experienced soldier and a commander of British forces. He had learned to handle hardships and had proven that he could overcome challenges.

Family and Government Duties

For two years after Cornwallis returned to England, he went to balls, invited friends to his estate, and enjoyed fox hunting. As he became more mature, he only attended parties or other social affairs when absolutely necessary. What he enjoyed most was the quiet country life of his estate, far from the hustle and bustle of London.

In the 1760s, he met Jemima Tullekin Jones, whose father was a professional soldier and a colonel in a regiment of foot guards. In those days, marriages were often arranged and based on money—members of wealthy families tended to marry members of other wealthy families. Although Jemima Jones did not come from a wealthy family, Charles Cornwallis married her in 1768 in a union that was based on mutual affection. Cornwallis and his wife had two children—a son, also named Charles, and a daughter named Mary.

14

Cornwallis was one of the youngest members of the House of Lords during the mid- and late 1760s. One of the main topics discussed in Parliament was how best to rule the American colonies, which grew increasingly restless each year over British tax policies and legislation. In addition to tax laws, Parliament and the king had also passed many laws that restricted the colonists' activities. The colonists had no voice in the Parliament, and could not join in the debate when the laws were passed.

Almost from the beginning, Cornwallis pitted himself against majority opinion. He voted against the Stamp Act of 1765, an English law that helped ignite rebellion in the colonies. As a means to collect taxes from the colonists, this law demanded that all printed documents produced in the colonies carry a stamp.

In 1766, after strong protests in the colonies,

Colonial newspapers printed protests such as this against the hated Stamp Act.

Parliament repealed the Stamp Act. At the same time, however, British lawmakers passed the Declaratory Act, which stated that England had the right to make laws for the colonies "in all cases whatsoever." In effect, the Declaratory Act made it illegal for the colonists to hold their own assemblies or to make any laws for themselves. Cornwallis was one of five members of the House of Lords who voted against the Declaratory Act. Throughout his time in Parliament, his sympathies— and votes—were on the side of the colonists.

Although Cornwallis often took stands against government policy, he was a close friend of King George III, who was Cornwallis's age and had taken the throne in 1760. Some historians believe that the king valued Cornwallis's honesty and openness. Whatever the reason, there were few men at court whom the king trusted as much as Cornwallis, and he served as aide-de-camp to the king for a year.

Beginning, in the late 1760s, Cornwallis took on many other roles in government. In 1771, he became vice-treasurer of Ireland and was sent to the city of Cork. At that time, Ireland was a colony of England. The country was governed by a parliament of Protestant landholders and appointees from England, including Cornwallis.

In April 1775, events in America changed the course of Cornwallis's life. On April 19, American colonists fought British regulars at Lexington and Concord in Massachusetts. These were the first

16

shots of the American Revolution. In response, George III immediately sent more British troops to stop the rebellion.

In March 1776, Cornwallis, at age 38, became a lieutenant general of the army of North America. Although Cornwallis had opposed the king's policies for the American colonies, duty to his country—and his king—was always foremost in his mind. Now duty called for him to leave Ireland and lead British troops to support the king's control over the American colonies.

In 1776, Cornwallis was sent to America to help his king maintain control of the colonies.

Chapter 2

EARLY YEARS OF
THE REVOLUTION

Although the British army was the most powerful in the world, England had no military academy to train officers. Most men became officers through wealth or the influence of friends. Because the richest classes were the landowners and the aristocracy, officers came mainly from those classes.

Men who wanted to become officers had to pay a great deal of money to receive commissions from the king—sometimes more than a poor person earned in a lifetime. Before an officer could purchase a commission for a higher rank, he had to serve a particular amount of time in the initial rank.

OPPOSITE: Cornwallis was third in command of the huge British force that landed on Long Island in New York, August 1776.

Charles Cornwallis

British troops, known as redcoats, had been used to put down revolts in Ireland and India.

When the war in the colonies began, Cornwallis volunteered to serve. The king was impressed that Cornwallis volunteered. Few officers who had served as long as Cornwallis would be willing to serve as third in command, a rather minor role. Most officers wanted the glory that came with being appointed first in command. George III had given that position to Sir William Howe. Sir Henry Clinton was Howe's second in command. Both men had begun their military careers by purchasing their ranks, and neither had the military education that Cornwallis had had in his youth.

In contrast to the officers, soldiers in the British army had little choice about their posts or their rank. Most soldiers came from the lower classes. They were volunteers who had no jobs, or men who wanted adventure and a chance to leave the grim circumstances of lower-class life behind.

Unlike Cornwallis, many British subjects refused to volunteer to fight in the American Revolution, because the Americans fought back so fiercely. British troops were more accustomed to subduing poor Irish peasants or unarmed subjects from India. As the enlistments declined, the army was allowed to take men from prison to fill out the ranks. Men who owed debts or even those in jail for serious crimes could earn their freedom if they served in the army. Even this approach failed to fill the ranks, so the British army took any man between the ages of 16 and 55 who stood at least five feet, three inches tall. There were still not enough men for the British army, and the king decided to pay Hessian soldiers from German states to meet his military needs.

British soldiers were trained to follow orders without question. Punishment for disobedience was hanging. Punishment for training mistakes or simple misbehavior might be as many as 1,000 whiplashes on the bare back.

During the mid-1700s, soldiers' uniforms varied slightly from regiment to regiment, but most members of the infantry wore red coats, white vests, and white breeches. Foot soldiers also carried pouches for ammunition slung over one shoulder and cartridge boxes over the other. On their backs, foot soldiers strapped a pack that contained a change of clothes, food, and canteens. They usually marched into battle with 60 pounds of equipment on their backs.

British soldiers carried a firearm called the Brown Bess. It was a smoothbore flintlock almost five feet long. The Brown Bess was not a precise weapon. It fired a one-ounce musket ball that was only accurate up to about 125 yards. The Brown Bess could not be fired in wet weather, because rain or snow would soak the powder in the priming pan. The Brown Bess, however, was very effective for one purpose. It could hold a bayonet—a two-foot-long, razor-sharp knife. Such charges—even the threat of a charge—accounted for the British success in many battles and skirmishes with the Crown's colonial subjects around the world.

In February 1776, Cornwallis left Cork, Ireland, and sailed for the Cape Fear River in North Carolina. Stormy weather delayed his arrival until May. Once in North Carolina, Cornwallis reported to the senior general, Clinton, who was an old acquaintance, several years older than Cornwallis.

Clinton was under orders to establish a Loyalist government in the Carolinas, which had a large number of people who still supported the king. Weeks before Cornwallis arrived, colonial Loyalists had lost a battle against Patriots at Moore's Creek Bridge.

Clinton and Cornwallis gave up on North Carolina and decided instead to march south and attack Charleston, South Carolina. The large port city was protected by Fort Moultrie, a small stronghold on Sullivan's Island at the entrance to the harbor. At the end of June 1776, the British anchored in the lower harbor.

Clinton and Cornwallis began the war on friendly terms.

Fort Moultrie guarded the passage between the lower and upper harbors. The city of Charleston was situated on the upper harbor. British leaders planned to land on Sullivan's Island and attack the fort from the rear, while the ships fired at the front of the fort.

Clinton launched the attack in an area north of Sullivan's Island. The troops were to wade across a shallow channel to the island. Clinton had been told that the channel was only about 18 inches deep, but he discovered that the water was really about 7 feet deep. He had no boats to take his soldiers across the channel. By the time he was able to send for some, the Americans had begun to fire artillery at their position.

23

About 200 redcoats, including many officers, were killed in the failed mission. As a result, Clinton and Cornwallis loaded their men on the warships and sailed north toward New York.

Chasing Washington

Clinton and Cornwallis arrived in New York in early August 1776 to join forces with William Howe, commander of the British army in America. Shortly after Cornwallis, about 8,400 Hessians and 26,000 British soldiers also arrived in New York. This brought the total British presence to about 35,000 troops. New York Harbor was crowded with more than 400 transport ships and a fleet of powerful warships manned by nearly 7,000 sailors. It was the largest force that England had ever sent overseas.

Unlike most generals in the British army, Cornwallis was well liked by his men, who felt great confidence in his leadership. He, in turn, was devoted to the welfare of his troops. "I have many friends in the American army [the British army in America], I love that army, and flatter myself that I am not quite indifferent to them," Cornwallis once said.

Cornwallis's troops realized that, unlike many other officers, their leader was a professional soldier who had studied his trade. He lived and marched with his men. He was also ahead of his time in his development of war games, which kept his men prepared to fight during the lulls between battles that occurred in the first year of the Revolution. He carried out these exercises in the same formal way that all fighting was done in Europe at that time. As he wrote, "In all marching, whether in column or line, it is absolutely necessary that the officer who is posted on the flank to which the troops are ordered to dress, should observe a steady & uniform pace, & that he should march perfectly straight.... In marching in column it is of the greatest consequence that the distances between the divisions should be observed with precision."

In August 1776, John Paul Jones was commissioned in Philadelphia as the captain of the American warship *Providence*.

★

The results of his training regimen were evident to other soldiers. An officer of the Ninth regiment, an infantry unit that was under the command of Clinton, observed the men trained under Cornwallis and wrote "I have felt a certain shamefacedness, on visiting...the 33rd Regiment... commanded by...Cornwallis, to compare...the steadiness of their discipline with the slovenly... bearing of most of our own companies....I have seen men go on duty in the 9th dead drunk and scarcely able to stand, but with the 33rd the sentry was always alert and alive in attention; when on duty, he was all eye, all ear."

Cornwallis believed that discipline was key to survival in war. He asked a great deal of his men and he set his standards high for them—as high as the standards that he set for himself. This philosophy made Cornwallis's troops some of the finest foot

25

soldiers to serve in America during the Revolution. Howe called the troops under Cornwallis "far Superior to any other Corps within my observation."

In response to the arrival of the enormous, experienced British force, General George Washington had split his Continental army into two parts, placing half of his force on the western end of Long Island and the remainder on Manhattan island. Washington had placed his troops on the Heights of Guan, a row of hills that ran from Gowanus Bay toward the tip of Long Island. Unfortunately for Washington, the British had thousands more troops on Long Island than did the Americans.

Howe planned to move his army through an eastern pass over the hills and then turn west to attack the American position. Washington had placed his men at various intervals along the passes between the heights. He had mistakenly left one pass almost unguarded—only five soldiers were stationed at Jamaica Pass.

To keep Washington off guard, Howe sent 5,000 men under Major General James Grant to attack on the American right flank at Gowanus Bay. Then he took most of his men and marched on the lightly guarded pass. Clinton commanded the advance troops, which quickly killed the five Americans. Cornwallis commanded reserve forces that supported Clinton's advance.

By the next morning, Howe had gone through Jamaica Pass and turned west. Grant opened fire

In the Battle of Long Island, many Patriot soldiers came under fire for the first time.

on the American right flank. Hessians attacked the American center. Cornwallis and Clinton charged from behind.

Suddenly, the Americans were under fire—many of them for the first time in their lives. Many Patriots panicked and fled. The only opposition to the British attack was mounted by Major General William Alexander, who was known by his Irish title, General Lord Stirling. With his 950 troops from Maryland, Stirling held out against Grant's 5,000 men until Cornwallis arrived with his regiment and a battalion of grenadiers to overwhelm the Americans.

Howe believed he had achieved an easy victory. He appeared to have Washington cornered—the American army had British forces in front of them and the East River behind. During the foggy night of August 29, however, Washington used boats to take his men out of Long Island, across the East River to Manhattan. The next morning, Howe, who had planned to finish off the American resistance, was surprised to find that the Patriots had slipped away.

Cornwallis, who did not have a leadership role in the New York campaign, rode with the British army to White Plains. It was there that Cornwallis and Clinton first argued, and the cracks in their relationship began to form. In the Battle of White Plains, Clinton was in charge of the rear guard that moved on to Dobbs Ferry, in an attempt to lure the Patriots into an attack. Clinton disagreed with the strategy and decided to take his troops elsewhere. He would have done so if Howe had not sent a message that demanded that Clinton follow orders.

After the battle, Clinton blurted out to Cornwallis, "I cannot bear to serve under [Howe] and had rather command three companies by myself than hold my post [as] I have done in his army." Cornwallis later told Howe what Clinton had said. It is difficult to say why Cornwallis did this. It may have been because Cornwallis respected Howe's leadership and felt it was his duty to the commander. Besides, as a trained military man, Cornwallis believed strongly that soldiers should follow orders, as he himself had done all his life. Clinton, on the other hand, had never studied military matters and, as an aristocrat who had purchased a commission, may have felt himself equal to Howe.

Clinton was also considered by many of his fellow officers to be emotionally unstable. After the death of his wife in 1772, he had entered a deep depression and remained in seclusion for nearly two years before he resumed his career.

Whatever the reason for Cornwallis's action, when Clinton discovered what Cornwallis had done, the two men engaged in a loud shouting match. Cornwallis eventually apologized, but the two men had by then developed a distrust of each other.

Washington, meanwhile, had crossed the Hudson River, and left the New York City area under British control. When the Americans retreated across the Hudson, Cornwallis captured Fort Washington, on the northwestern edge of Manhattan, where Washington had left more than 2,800 men to stall the British. It was one of the largest captures of American prisoners during the war.

Across the Hudson River in New Jersey stood Fort Lee, which was held by about 4,000 American soldiers under the command of Nathanael Greene. Their job was to keep the British at bay while the majority of the American army hurried across the state toward Philadelphia. On November 19, Clinton sent Cornwallis and 4,500 men to defeat the Americans at Fort Lee. Cornwallis took his men across the Hudson River to the Jersey shore. The Americans were alerted to the approaching British, and left hurriedly. Cornwallis captured a huge supply of food, weapons, and tents that the Americans had left behind.

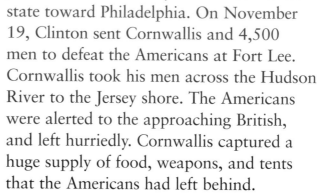

★

In November 1776, Thomas Paine was among the American soldiers who left Fort Lee when Cornwallis approached.

★

Once on the New Jersey side of the Hudson River, Cornwallis had the freedom to act independently. Clinton and Howe had remained in Manhattan, to establish order in the city, which had been largely destroyed by a fire believed to have been set by Patriots who wanted to deny supplies to the redcoats.

Washington and his army had marched south across New Jersey. Cornwallis decided to chase and defeat the Americans. On November 25, Cornwallis left Fort Lee with nine fresh battalions. On November 28, he entered Newark, New Jersey, just as the last of Washington's troops left. The British kept up the relentless pursuit and on December 1, they marched more than 20 miles over frozen roads to reach New Brunswick. Once again, Washington had just left the village.

Cornwallis finally had to stop at New Brunswick. His soldiers had marched on muddy roads for three days in the rain with 60-pound packs on their backs and only flour to eat. Eventually, his supply wagons fell so far behind that Cornwallis received orders from Howe to stop at the Raritan River. "I could not have pursued the enemy from Brunswick with any prospect of material advantage, or without greatly distressing the troops under my command," Cornwallis later wrote.

On December 6, Howe joined Cornwallis and took command. Together, they began to pursue the American army again. As darkness fell, the redcoats arrived in Princeton, New Jersey, about an hour after Washington's rear guard had pulled out of the village.

Howe ordered his men to make camp in the village and allowed them to sleep in comfort in the buildings of the College of New Jersey, later Princeton University. At nine o'clock the next morning, the British troops marched toward Trenton.

At about two o'clock in the afternoon, the British arrived in Trenton, just as the last of Washington's troops crossed the icy Delaware River to the Pennsylvania side. Washington had used most of the available boats and destroyed any that he did not use. Once again, Howe and Cornwallis had arrived too late.

With Washington's army in a safe position across the Delaware, Howe decided to return to his winter quarters in New York City. Howe's orders for December 14, 1776, stated that Cornwallis's

Hessian soldiers were feared by the untrained American troops.

actions had forced the Americans to flee across
New Jersey and had closed the British campaign
for the year "much to the honor of his lordship

32

[Cornwallis] and the Officers and Soldiers under his command." Howe spread a series of outposts across New Jersey, including Hessian troops that he posted at Trenton and Bordentown.

When Cornwallis arrived in New York City, he received word that his wife was ill. He requested a leave from Howe to return to England. At the same time, Howe received word that Washington had carried out a surprise attack on the Hessians at Trenton. The Americans had marched through a horrible winter storm to defeat the Hessians there on the day after Christmas.

Howe denied Cornwallis's request for leave and immediately ordered him to return to New Jersey and take command of the efforts to defeat the Continental army there. On New Year's Day 1777, Cornwallis traveled the 50 miles from New York to Princeton, and arrived late in the evening. He quickly organized soldiers into regiments—a total of about 8,000 regulars and a large artillery force—and prepared to march them to Trenton.

With little rest, Cornwallis started off with his army before dawn on January 2. Before he left, he placed a rear guard of 1,200 men under the command of Colonel Charles Mawhood at Princeton. At Maidenhead, New Jersey, he left another 1,500 men under General Alexander Leslie. Then, with the remainder of his troops, he moved toward Trenton.

Washington waited for Cornwallis at Trenton with 5,000 men. The American general had also placed men with long rifles along the Princeton-Trenton road. These expert marksmen hid behind trees and picked off British soldiers as they marched.

Marching was especially difficult because a January thaw and recent heavy rains had turned the roads into a swampy muck. One British soldier later reported, "The men sank halfway to their knees. The guns continually threatened to bog down. . . . At every turn of the road, from every flanking thicket and ravine, the bullets whistled . . . [then] the opposition simply melted away and had to be dealt with afresh at the next natural obstacle."

It took a full day for the British to march a distance of only 10 miles to Trenton. While he waited for Cornwallis, Washington formed a line on a ridge across from Trenton along the south bank of the Assunpunk Creek.

At about five o'clock that evening, Cornwallis arrived at Trenton. His tired troops attacked the Americans who held a bridge over the creek, but they could not get across. Twice Cornwallis ordered his men to try to cross the bridge, but they were stopped, and the creek soon ran red with British blood.

That evening, Cornwallis met with his generals. Sir William Erskine, the quartermaster general, said that the troops should attack that night. Other generals argued that the Americans were trapped. Because their boats were above Trenton, they could not get to them easily. Therefore, the Americans

34

were obviously not going anywhere and would still be in position the next morning. By then, the British would be rested and ready for battle.

Cornwallis was undecided. The right flank of the American army was exposed, but to attack, he would have to march his exhausted men over soggy ground in the dark. He also considered an attack from the front, but that strategy meant that his tired troops would have to cross a swollen stream in total darkness. Cornwallis told his generals that he would "bag the fox"—capture Washington—in the morning, and he ordered his men to set up camp.

Once again, however, Washington slipped out of the trap while the British campfires burned. He set up his own campfires and left 400 men to tend to them. Then he had his troops wrap cloth around the wheels of his artillery wagons and move out in absolute silence around the flank of the sleeping British troops. The next morning, Cornwallis awoke to discover that the Americans had slipped past him and were headed back toward Princeton in the same direction he had come.

Washington marched his men through the night to Princeton, where his troops defeated Mawhood's soldiers. From there, Washington wanted to move on to New Brunswick, where the British had stored ammunition and weapons, but his scouts informed him that Cornwallis was on the march toward Princeton. Washington wanted to avoid a head-on confrontation with the larger British force, and

35

Washington's triumph over Cornwallis at Princeton infuriated Howe and Clinton.

withdrew his men to winter quarters at Morristown, a wooded, hilly area north of Trenton and Princeton.

Howe was enraged by Washington's success and believed Cornwallis had committed a terrible blunder. Later, Clinton, who took the opportunity to get back at Cornwallis for the incident at White Plains, agreed with Howe, and said that Cornwallis had been guilty "of the most consummate ignorance I ever heard of [in] any officer above a corporal."

Chapter 3

WAR IN THE
MIDDLE STATES

In the spring of 1777, Howe changed his strategy. Up until this point, he had chased Washington, but now he would try to capture Philadelphia instead. He believed that if he could take the colonial capital—and the Continental Congress—he would demoralize the Americans. He left Clinton with 7,000 men in Manhattan. Howe sailed south along the coast and up the Chesapeake Bay to Philadelphia with a force of nearly 15,000 men.

OPPOSITE: Throughout the war, Washington commanded directly in the battlefield rather than from headquarters, in order to rally the American troops.

Charles Cornwallis

As the main meeting place of the Continental Congress, Philadelphia was at the very center of the American Revolution.

Cornwallis, who had been named second-in-command for the mission, marched across New Jersey from his winter camp in New Brunswick with a force of about 3,000 men to join forces with Howe. On April 13, 1777, he encountered a Patriot force under General Benjamin Lincoln in the small village of Bound Brook, New Jersey. Cornwallis's overwhelming superiority in numbers allowed him to defeat the smaller Patriot force, which lost 30 men before it retreated.

Howe expected Washington to fight fiercely in defense of Philadelphia. To ensure his own victory, Howe not only ordered Cornwallis to march across New Jersey, he also ordered General John Burgoyne to march down from Canada to capture Albany. With Burgoyne in control of Albany and

40

his own troops dominating Philadelphia, Howe believed he could crush the American force between the two British armies.

In late August, Howe arrived at Head of Elk, Pennsylvania, in the northern Chesapeake Bay. When Washington realized that the British objective was Philadelphia, he moved his troops south to stop the advance. He positioned 11,000 soldiers on the east side of Brandywine Creek, about halfway to Philadelphia.

Washington divided his men into three divisions and placed them along Brandywine Creek. Greene commanded the center division. Militia troops from Pennsylvania on Washington's left were expected to defend Chadds Ford on the main road to Philadelphia. This was the point at which Washington expected the British to cross the creek.

Washington posted another division, under General John Sullivan, on his right, slightly upstream of Chadds Ford. If the British tried to flank the Americans, Sullivan's troops would be a line of defense. Unfortunately for the Americans, Washington did not place Sullivan far enough upstream.

On September 11, Howe sent half of his troops under General Wilhelm von Knyphausen directly to Chadds Ford. He planned to use this attack as a diversion to make the Americans think his whole army would cross the creek there.

Howe and Cornwallis took the remainder of the army to the north. The plan was for Cornwallis to

41

cross the creek to the north—far above Sullivan—then bear down on the rear of the American right flank.

About 4 A.M. on September 11, Howe and Cornwallis led their combined force north to the creek. By early afternoon, British soldiers were poised to attack the American right flank.

The Americans were completely surprised. British soldiers fired volley after volley from two lines of riflemen, while they kept another line in reserve. Sullivan, aware of the danger he was in, tried to form his troops to meet the attack head on. As Sullivan started to form his line on a hill right across from the redcoats' attack, Cornwallis opened fire with his artillery.

Cannonballs and canister shot blasted the American ranks as the British infantry stood ready to charge. Guards on the right, grenadiers in the center, and Hessian soldiers on the left stood with their bayonets gleaming in the sunlight. In their bright red uniforms and gold lace, Cornwallis and Howe sat on their horses and watched the destruction of the American forces.

At 4 P.M., Howe and Cornwallis gave the soldiers an order to charge. A band played the "British

William Howe commanded the forces that defeated the Patriots at Brandywine.

Grenadiers" anthem. The column marched forward in a disciplined charge, their bayonets raised.

Most of Sullivan's troops fled in terror, though some of the Americans fought the British hand to hand. Sullivan's force would have been destroyed if Greene had not marched his men four miles in 45 minutes, despite terrible heat, to protect Sullivan's wounded men as they retreated.

At Chadds Ford, Knyphausen carried out his attack, in which he sent his men across the Brandywine and forced the Americans back. In the battle, redcoats captured most of the American artillery. Only darkness, which allowed the Americans to slip into the surrounding forests, prevented a massacre.

The British victory at Brandywine was diminished in early October by news of Burgoyne's loss. At Saratoga, New York, an American force under General Benedict Arnold had defeated the British in one of the key engagements of the war. It was this battle that convinced France that the Americans had a chance to win the war. Plans were set in motion for an alliance between France and the new United States.

After the battle at Brandywine, the British entered Philadelphia, but Cornwallis did not stay there long. Soon after he helped to direct the fortification of the city, he was reassigned. By the middle of November, he was in command of one of the forts along the Delaware that Howe had set up to protect the supply route to Philadelphia.

As winter approached, Cornwallis knew that there would not be much fighting until the next spring. He again asked Howe for leave to return to England and care for his wife. This time, Howe granted the request.

On December 16, Cornwallis sailed for home. He arrived in England in the middle of January 1778, and immediately went to his estate. There was little he could do for his wife, who had been bedridden for almost a year and was slowly dying from tuberculosis, a respiratory ailment. For the next three months, he took care of personal matters and visited the families of some fellow officers. He also met with government officials to relate the progress of the war. Because he was still a member of the House of Lords, he also attended some of Parliament's sessions.

During these sessions, the British government decided to attempt to make peace with the colonies. The Parliament was prepared to repeal all laws it had passed since 1763 and allow the colonies a limited form of self-rule. A group of peace commissioners planned to sail to America to begin negotiations. The commissioners agreed to bring Cornwallis along on their ship.

The commission, known as the Carlisle Commission, arrived in New York City in the spring of 1778. Before they were able to present their offer to the Continental Congress in Philadelphia, however, word reached the Americans that a treaty of alliance had been signed with

44

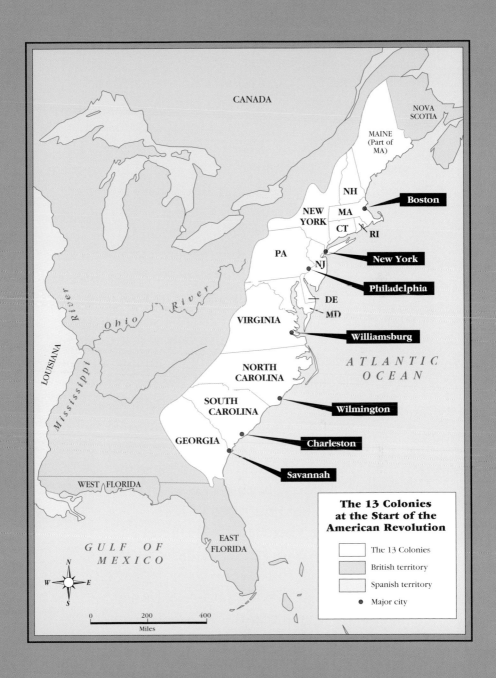

CANADA

NOVA
SCOTIA

MAINE
(Part of
MA)

NH

NEW
YORK

MA

CT

RI

Boston

PA

NJ

New York

Philadelphia

DE

MD

VIRGINIA

Williamsburg

ATLANTIC
OCEAN

NORTH
CAROLINA

SOUTH
CAROLINA

Wilmington

GEORGIA

Charleston

Savannah

WEST FLORIDA

LOUISIANA

Mississippi River

Ohio River

EAST
FLORIDA

GULF OF
MEXICO

N
W E
S

**The 13 Colonies
at the Start of the
American Revolution**

The 13 Colonies

British territory

Spanish territory

● Major city

0   200   400

Miles

France. Congress then voted to refrain from any negotiations with England that did not offer complete independence.

By June 1778, Cornwallis had reached the Delaware River. A few days later, he arrived in Philadelphia. By this time, Howe was no longer the commander of the British forces in America. He had sent his resignation to the English government the previous October after Burgoyne's defeat at Saratoga. In February 1778, the government promoted Henry Clinton to command the British forces. Cornwallis became second in command.

Despite the disagreement of the past years, Cornwallis still valued his relationship with Clinton. As a career military man, Cornwallis also believed strongly in obedience to the chain of command, which required him to follow orders without question even if he disagreed with a military strategy. When he learned that Clinton had been promoted, Cornwallis wrote to him, "I will do all in my power to contribute to your ease in a situation which I fear you will not find a bed of roses."

> ★
> In early 1778, John Adams began a dangerous three-month ocean journey to France, where he served as American minister to the French.
> ★

By the time Cornwallis arrived in Philadelphia, Clinton received orders from Parliament to move his troops back to New York City. Cornwallis strongly disagreed with that order. A man of action, he figured that the British and Americans would remain in a stalemate in New York, and he would see no more fighting. Two weeks later,

Charles Cornwallis

however, he found himself in the thick of a very hot battle—the Battle of Monmouth.

The Final Battle in the North

On June 18, Clinton's huge force began its march from Philadelphia toward New York. More than 10,000 men with baggage, wagons, horses, hospital supplies, boats, bridges, bakeries, laundries, and blacksmith shops on wheels formed a parade 12 miles long. Clinton planned to meet the navy at Sandy Hook, New Jersey, and then sail north to New York.

In pursuit of the British army was Washington, with about 13,000 men. The Americans hoped to take advantage of the slow-moving redcoats and harass them before they made it to the British stronghold in New York City. Near the town of Monmouth in eastern New Jersey, Clinton divided his troops into two divisions. The advance division, with all the baggage, was commanded by Knyphausen. Cornwallis brought up the rear division.

Washington developed a plan to attack the British rear guard. He believed that if he attacked the rear, the advance division would be unable to come to Cornwallis's aid because of all its baggage. Thus, on the brutally hot, humid day of June 28, the British and American forces fought their last battle in the north.

The American vanguard of about 4,000 soldiers was commanded by General Charles Lee. Near Monmouth, Lee fought about 2,000 British soldiers of Cornwallis's rear guard. Cornwallis's troops were joined by about 4,000 men under Clinton's command.

At the beginning of the battle, Clinton and Cornwallis's troops forced Lee's men back through rough terrain. Lee's soldiers ran in terror at the advance of the British troops. Clinton moved in fast pursuit, because he feared that Lee's soldiers would be able to join with Washington's main army. The redcoats, in their woolen uniforms, were at a great disadvantage in the 96-degree heat. Many dropped dead from heatstroke during the chase and fight.

Finally, the pursuit ended, and the Americans turned to meet their enemies. Clinton's charge against the Americans on the left was repulsed. Then Clinton sent Cornwallis and his crack British infantry against Greene on the right.

This charge went into the jaws of an artillery battery commanded by Henry Knox, whose ability to fire cannons with pinpoint accuracy had become almost legendary during the siege of Boston in 1775. As Cornwallis ordered his men to charge, the formidable line of Knox's American cannons opened fire. A British soldier later reported, "One round shot struck the muskets from the hands of an entire platoon."

Cornwallis's men fell, yet he ordered others behind them to continue the charge. His men held their bayonets up to strike—a pose that usually intimidated the Americans. This time, however,

48

Washington's soldiers stood their ground, and fired round after round into the redcoats as they charged.

It soon became evident that Cornwallis could not defeat the Americans. The solid line of British soldiers suddenly broke and scattered. He ordered his men to retreat. Clinton then ordered all of his army to a defensive position behind a ravine.

The battle, which had lasted for most of the day, was over by 6:00 P.M. Washington knew that he could not attack the British position, and both armies were too tired to continue the fight. Almost as many men had fallen dead from heatstroke as had been cut down by cannon and musket fire. Clinton's men rested until midnight, then moved toward Sandy Hook.

Although the Battle of Monmouth was a stand-off between the British and American forces, it renewed the underlying tension between Cornwallis, the trained military commander, and Clinton, the wealthy noble who had bought his way up through the ranks. Cornwallis felt that the decision to send his men against Greene and Knox—Clinton's order—was suicidal and could only have been given by someone who did not understand military strategy. Yet, true to his training, Cornwallis had obeyed his superior and done all in his power to break the Patriots' resistance. Nevertheless, Clinton gave Cornwallis little praise for his charge, and gave only a brief mention in the battle report of his "zealous services."

Chapter 4

THE BRITISH
TURN SOUTH

As the summer of 1778 wore on, Cornwallis grew weary of the inactive camp life at New York City. Then, in the fall, he received word that his wife was near death in England. Because Clinton had no campaign planned against the Americans, he gave Cornwallis leave to return home. As the general left, he intended to resign his commission.

In December 1778, Cornwallis arrived in London and relayed Clinton's request for more soldiers to the government. He also turned in his resignation—which the king accepted—before he hurried to his estate.

OPPOSITE: London was one of the wealthiest cities in the world during the 1700s.

Cornwallis found that his wife's long battle with tuberculosis was in its final stage. Throughout January and much of February, he tried to nurse her back to health, and never left the estate. He wrote to Clinton in January, "The very ill...health in which I found Lady Cornwallis has render'd me incapable of any attention but to her."

On February 14, 1779, Jemima Cornwallis died. Although he was by nature a calm person, Cornwallis broke down completely at his wife's death. For weeks, he refused to talk to or see anyone. He was in deep mourning, and wrote to his brother that his wife's death had "destroyed all my hopes of happiness in this world."

Back into Service

Finally, to take his mind off his wife's death, Cornwallis returned to service in the army. On April 14, 1779, he wrote to Clinton to discuss the possibility of his return to America. He had no desire for command, he wrote, but he wished to take up arms for his country once again.

Cornwallis wrote that if Clinton had plans to fight in the south, he would "with great pleasure come out & meet you." Then, in a reference to his loss, he wrote, "This country has now no charms for me, & I am perfectly indifferent as to what part of the world I may go."

The king accepted Cornwallis's offer to return to America. In May, Cornwallis wrote to his brother, "I am now returning to America not with views of conquest and ambition, nothing brilliant can be expected in that quarter; but I find this country quite unsupportable to me. I must shift the scene."

When Clinton learned that Cornwallis was about to return to America, he wrote an appreciative letter to officials in the British government: "I must beg leave to express how happy I am made by the return of Lord Cornwallis to this country. His lordship's indefatigable Zeal, his knowledge of the Country, his professional Ability, and the high estimation in which he is held by this Army . . . give me . . . confidence of . . . support from him." Cornwallis returned to America in July 1779. He landed in New York City to learn that the war in the north was still in a stalemate.

By this time, Clinton had turned his attention to the southern colonies. Like many British military leaders, he believed that there was strong Loyalist sentiment in the south. With the numbers of regular troops dwindling and reinforcements slow to arrive from England, Clinton felt that his best chance for success was to form a large militia among southern colonists.

> ★
>
> In September 1779, the *Bonhomme Richard* under Captain John Paul Jones defeated the British ship *Serapis* in the largest naval battle of the Revolution.
>
> ★

In December 1779, Clinton left 10,000 troops in New York under Knyphausen to defend against a possible American attack. Then he and Cornwallis loaded about 8,500 soldiers on 14 warships and sailed south to launch an attack on Charleston, South Carolina—the same place where they had been defeated in 1776.

It took more than a month in icy winter seas for the British transports to reach Savannah, Georgia, about 30 miles south of Charleston. Once in Georgia, Clinton and Cornwallis solidified their plan to lay siege to Charleston. The key was to take control of the Ashley River to the west of Charleston and the Cooper River to the east. This would trap American commander Benjamin Lincoln and his force of 5,500 soldiers and militia in the city.

As word of the coming British attack spread, South Carolina governor John Rutledge had slaves build new forts across the neck between the rivers. He also ordered four American warships to be sunk at the mouth of the Cooper River to provide a barrier across the river.

On March 29, 1780, Clinton and Cornwallis crossed into South Carolina with more than 10,000 regulars and loyalist militia. On April 8, eight British ships dropped anchor in Charleston harbor. Soon, the city was almost surrounded on both land and water. British guns opened fire on April 13.

While Cornwallis waited with his force in reserve, Clinton led his troops forward. By April 19, the British were within 200 yards of the American forces inside the city. Lincoln tried to arrange an agreement with Clinton that would allow the American soldiers to leave Charleston in an honorable way, with arms shouldered and flags raised. Clinton refused, because he realized that he

Charleston was the largest port on the East Coast south of Philadelphia.

was in a position to take the city and capture the American army at the same time.

On May 6, a group of British marines took over Fort Moultrie in Charleston Harbor. Two days later, the British army was ready to launch a final assault. Before he gave the command to attack, Clinton asked Lincoln to surrender. Lincoln refused unless his force was allowed to surrender with honor. Clinton's reply was to launch an artillery barrage that continued for several days and nights.

The Charleston city government had originally supported Lincoln's efforts to save the city. When the artillery barrage started several large fires in the city, however, they reversed their stand and asked Lincoln to surrender. On May 12, the American soldiers surrendered. The entire American force, about 5,500 regulars and militia, were confined to a prison camp. Now, the British had a base that could be easily supplied by sea and from which they could strike at the southern interior.

55

Chapter 5

COMMAND IN THE SOUTH

Though Cornwallis had carried out important support actions at Charleston, he had seen little direct action. The tension that had existed between him and Clinton since their campaign in New York City, when Cornwallis had told Howe of Clinton's insult, had returned. When Clinton decided to return to New York in June, Cornwallis eagerly took command of the southern forces, pleased to be on his own, at least to a certain extent, with Clinton far to the north.

OPPOSITE: The Battle of Camden was a discouraging loss for the Patriots.

Before he returned to New York, Clinton gave specific orders. Cornwallis could direct his forces where he thought best and could attack or withdraw as he saw fit, as long as he maintained control over Savannah and Charleston. He could also provide supplies for his troops from the local farms, a practice that the British usually tried to avoid.

Cornwallis was instructed to move into North Carolina after he had taken control of South Carolina. Then, after he established forts to maintain control of both states, he was to move on to Virginia. Clinton's instructions were clear. How to carry them out, however, was completely unclear.

Cornwallis faced multiple tasks. He had to set up governments that would be loyal to England, recruit Loyalist militia units, man forts in the interior, make sure his troops had food and tents, and prepare for a possible attack from the Continental army. His biggest problem was that Clinton had left him with very few troops and funds to carry out these orders.

It took Cornwallis a month to put his strategy into operation. To place soldiers at strategic points, however, was easier than to supply them or communicate with them. Keeping troops supplied with weapons, ammunition, uniforms, and food was a maddening process. Those items were shipped from England to New York before they were sent on to Cornwallis. Clinton, who was plagued with worry that New York City would come under siege, was slow to send supplies in case he might need them. In several cases, small American warships captured the British supply ships.

Even supplies that were unloaded at Charleston still had to be taken to the army posts. The South Carolina roads were rutted and the summer rains turned them into muddy bogs. It was impossible to use rivers for transport because the heavy rains caused them to overflow.

Because food was so slow to arrive from New York, Cornwallis had to depend on the food that was available in the countryside. At first, the British found large supplies of food at captured locations, but within weeks, those supplies were exhausted. Cornwallis then tried to buy food supplies from Loyalists. As loyal as these Americans were, they charged extremely high prices for their food, and Clinton had not provided Cornwallis with enough funds to purchase food for the troops.

In August 1780, Cornwallis reached the outskirts of Camden, South Carolina, with about 3,000 men. There, he received information that General Horatio Gates had been placed in charge of the American army in the south and that Gates had started to march toward Camden. Cornwallis was pleased to have a chance to fight and perhaps destroy a large American force.

Cornwallis set up his headquarters in a large house owned by Joseph Kershaw, a merchant and

★

In August 1780, a French force of 5,000 men, including a large cavalry unit, landed in Rhode Island.

★

Patriot. It gave Cornwallis pleasure to punish Kershaw and set an example for others who supported the American cause. He allowed Kershaw's wife and children to stay in an upper room, but he sent Kershaw to Bermuda as a prisoner of war.

The first spy reports stated that Gates's army was made up of about 5,000 soldiers. Cornwallis did not believe that Gates could have an army that large, but he was still concerned because his own force had just 3,000 men. On August 14, Cornwallis inspected his troops and tried to decide whether to face Gates or return to Charleston.

By then, Cornwallis had received word that Thomas Sumter, a Patriot guerrilla leader, was camped behind him on the Wateree River. Throughout the summer, Sumter had led his men against British outposts, while he recruited ever larger numbers of local fighters.

Finally, Cornwallis decided against a retreat to Charleston. He believed that if he defeated Gates and Sumter, people in South Carolina would be convinced that the British were going to establish control over their state.

Cornwallis desperately needed a thriving city such as Camden to be under British control. Camden's factories could provide military supplies for his soldiers. Tea, corn, rum, bacon, ham, butter, and tobacco were produced in the surrounding countryside. He could find cattle and sheep to feed his men. There were also some Loyalist merchants to provide support as the British set up a new government and started a loyalist militia.

In mid-August, Cornwallis sent a spy to infiltrate Gates's forces, which had marched to Rugely's Mill, about 10 miles north of Camden, and set up a base camp for the anticipated battle. The spy pretended to be a militiaman from Maryland. He carefully studied the size of Gates's force and the quantity of its supplies.

The spy returned to the British camp with the news that Gates had about 3,000 men. Cornwallis had about the same number of men, but only about 2,000 were healthy enough to fight. The others were ill from malaria and other diseases that were common in the swampy regions of the south. Although he was outnumbered, what Cornwallis did not realize was that a large number of the American troops were inexperienced. Gates's only experienced fighters were the Delaware and Maryland regulars—about 1,000 soldiers.

In the American camp, Gates had concerns of his own about whether to take on the British. Several weeks earlier, before he had started on the march toward the Camden area, he had been warned by local residents that the South Carolina countryside was "barren, abounding in sandy plains, intersected by swamps, sparsely inhabited, and capable of furnishing but little provisions and forage."

During the march to Rugely's Mill, the American soldiers lived on nothing but unripe apples and peaches. Officers had some soup to eat, but it was so watery that they used the hair powder that was used on wigs to thicken it. On August 3, Gates's men had met up with more than 2,000 North Carolina militia. This group nearly doubled the size of Gates's army, but the march through the pine barrens had weakened his men.

Cornwallis started north from Camden to meet Gates on August 15. On the American side, Gates who had come to believe that the addition of militia would enable him to defeat the British, ordered his men to leave Rugely's Mill and march toward Camden that night. Five miles north of Camden, the two armies met on the night of August 16, which surprised both Gates and Cornwallis.

As Cornwallis led his main force toward Gates, the sound of gunfire came through the dark. The British advance guard had run head-on into Gates's advance guard. Cornwallis quickly ordered his men to halt and form battle lines across both sides of the road, but he refused to attack because of the darkness.

The land where the opposing forces stopped favored the British style of open-field, arranged-formation fighting. Swamps on their right and left would prevent an American attack on their flanks from behind cover. Cornwallis decided to set up camp and wait for morning light before he attacked.

Gates, who had expected to encounter a small British force, had suddenly encountered a large army. When he learned that the British army numbered about 2,000 soldiers and was led by Cornwallis, Gates became doubtful of the chances of his own raw force.

The morning of August 16 was hot and hazy. Cornwallis stared through the early morning mist at his enemy, about 250 yards ahead. As soon as enemy shapes could be made out, both sides opened fire. Soon the smoke of battle hung in the still air.

Immediately, Cornwallis saw an opening at the American left and center, where the Virginia and North Carolina militia were stationed. He had sent a small group of infantry opposite these men, along with his crack 33rd Regiment. The American right seemed to be more powerful, so Cornwallis assaulted it with a larger force of Irish volunteers and infantry.

> ★
>
> In the summer of 1780, the University of Pennsylvania awarded an honorary Master of Arts degree to Thomas Paine for his writing.
>
> ★

Gates's first order was to have the Virginia militia attack the British right. The Virginians tried to charge with their bayonets raised, but were untrained in the use of bayonets in battle. The British turned their own bayonets against the Virginians and slaughtered them. They followed with a volley of fire toward the Virginia militia, who threw down their guns and ran into the swamps.

Gates had made a great error in his battle plan. He had placed his Continental troops—the only experienced men he had—on the right and the Virginia and North Carolina militia on the left,

63

with no support from the Continentals. The British charge into the American left side had caused the American battle line to collapse.

Once they got through the line, Cornwallis's troops turned right into the left flank of the Continentals. The American militia fought back valiantly, though they had no support. Two regiments of Americans were destroyed, and those that were not killed ran from the field of battle, leaving muskets and artillery behind.

The Americans suffered more than 800 killed and captured. Gates himself fled from the battle, and rode as fast as he could to Charlotte, North Carolina, before he stopped. When Colonel Alexander Hamilton, Washington's chief aide, heard of Gates's action, he commented, "Was there ever such an instance of a general running away... from his whole army?"

It had taken Cornwallis only an hour to defeat the largest American force in the south. One observer described the scene, "The road for some miles was strewed with the wounded and killed.... The number of dead horses, broken wagons, and baggage scattered on the road formed a perfect scene of horror and confusion... such was the terror and dismay of the Americans."

After the battle, Cornwallis reaped a great bounty. He had captured all the American artillery, which included seven brass cannons. The British now had what the Americans had brought with them—150 supply wagons, baggage, camp equipment, 20

64

wagons full of ammunition, and most of the muskets that the men had carried.

Not satisfied with his victory over Gates, Cornwallis decided to finish off Thomas Sumter as well. He sent Lieutenant Colonel Banastre Tarleton after Sumter. Tarleton was the feared leader of the horseback unit called the British Legion. A ruthless attacker, Tarleton had helped demolish Gates's soldiers, and even followed the wounded and killed them.

On August 18, Tarleton caught up with Sumter and his men south of Camden. The British cavalry attacked, and hacked with their sabers until they destroyed the enemy force. Tarleton's force killed 150 men and took 300 prisoners. They also captured 2 brass cannons and 44 wagons.

Cornwallis and the British soldiers were stunned by the ease of their victory. Cornwallis was so pleased that he sent an aide to England with the news. For weeks, Cornwallis's victory was the main topic of discussion among the British military command in New York City, and Cornwallis was seen as the major military figure in America. He began to feel as though it would be only a matter of time before he controlled the southern colonies.

Cornwallis was happy to be the center of attention, but he also knew that popularity of this kind was fleeting, especially within the British military. For that reason, he wanted to finish off all resistance in the Carolinas quickly. From there, it would be a simple matter to capture the warehouses and port cities of Virginia.

After Cornwallis defeated Gates's army, he was confident that Georgia and South Carolina were under British control. He turned his sights toward North Carolina and began to organize wagons and supplies for the march.

Yet Cornwallis continued to be harassed by the local Patriots. It was difficult for the British to fight against soldiers who engaged in guerrilla warfare. These fighters ambushed the redcoats while they marched, and shot at the British from behind trees. Using hit-and- run tactics, the Americans often set fire to the British camps or destroyed trains of supply wagons.

Patriots in the border area between North and South Carolina also terrorized Loyalists and destroyed their homes, businesses, and plantations so they would not help the British. Attacks became especially brutal in the western border areas between the states. There, frontiersmen used hit-and-run attacks on Loyalists and on the British outposts that had been built to protect the Loyalists. As the fall of 1780 approached, Cornwallis realized that these guerrilla raids threatened his control of South Carolina, as well as his campaign into North Carolina.

To stop the raids, Cornwallis decided to send a unit to end the fighting in the western counties as he started his own march north to Charlotte, North Carolina. He chose Major Patrick Ferguson to lead the mission. Ferguson seemed to have a natural gift for recruiting men to fight under him, and had assembled a large unit of Loyalist militia in South Carolina.

Ferguson and his men entered the western area of South Carolina in late September. As they marched, the force spread the word that if the colonists did not lay down their weapons, the Loyalists would "lay the country waste with fire and sword." Residents of the area were enraged at these threats. A Patriot militia made up of sharpshooting woodsmen soon gathered to oppose Ferguson's unit. About 900 frontiersmen assembled in early October and set out to attack Ferguson.

When Ferguson learned that the frontiersmen were on their way toward him, he set up his men at Kings Mountain, North Carolina, just over the border from South Carolina. Located in the foothills of the Great Smoky Mountains, King's Mountain is a high point shaped like a bootprint.

On October 7, Ferguson's group of about 1,100 Loyalists met a force of 900 crackshot riflemen. As the frontiersmen moved silently up through the woods, they blended in with their surroundings. Hidden behind the thick trees, they opened fire. Ferguson organized his men to make a disciplined bayonet charge. They drove one group of frontiersmen back, but the frontiersmen rallied and returned to fire on Ferguson again. From their hiding places, the frontiersmen easily picked off the Loyalists.

★

In September 1780, Benedict Arnold, the hero of the American victory at Saratoga in 1777, went over to the British side.

★

Charles Cornwallis

Patriot militia routed British major Patrick Ferguson and a loyalist force at King's Mountain.

Ferguson had his men charge twice more, in an attempt to drive the frontiersmen back. Yet the frontiersmen continued to shoot from the dark undergrowth with quick and deadly fire from their long rifles, which were much more accurate than the British weapons. Many of the Americans put four or five musket balls into their mouths, so they

Charles Cornwallis

could rapidly spit them into the gun barrel, then reload and shoot.

Ferguson dashed from soldier to soldier to encourage each man to fight. Atop his white horse, he waved his sword to order his men to attack. Suddenly, a volley of musket fire hit Ferguson and he dropped.

As soon as Ferguson died, the Loyalists tried to surrender, but the frontiersmen continued to fire. Finally, their leader, Colonel Isaac Shelby, ordered the shooting to stop and gathered more than 700 Loyalist prisoners. Later, some of the Loyalists were tried as traitors and hanged. Ferguson was the only British officer killed in the battle. The rest were Americans—225 Loyalists and 28 Patriots.

The defeat at Kings Mountain left Cornwallis's left flank vulnerable to attack. Because the thick forests of that region left his men at a disadvantage in fighting style, Cornwallis decided to delay his campaign against Charlotte in central North Carolina. Instead, he fell back to Winnsboro, in western South Carolina, where he set up winter quarters. The open landscape allowed him to establish supply lines from Charleston without

69

concern about raids from the colonials hidden in the woods. After the death of the popular Ferguson, the British were never again successful in their attempts to raise a Loyalist militia. When Clinton heard of the defeat, he said he hoped that it was not "the first link in a chain of evils."

In December 1780, Washington sent the experienced and reliable Nathanael Greene to command what remained of Gates's southern force. The Continental army then consisted of about 1,500 men who were healthy enough to fight. Greene sent 600 men from the base camp at Deep River, North Carolina, to the western border region under the command of Daniel Morgan, and took the remainder of his troops southeast to Cheraw Hill, South Carolina, where supplies were more readily available.

General Nathanael Greene became one of Washington's most trusted commanders during the Revolution.

Charles Cornwallis

From his winter quarters in Winnsboro, Cornwallis sent Tarleton and 1,100 of his cavalry to attack Morgan. On January 12, 1781, Tarleton started in pursuit of Morgan and his small force.

Outnumbered, Morgan fell back. The British horsemen moved quickly, however, and Tarleton was soon only 10 miles behind the Americans near the town of Cowpens, South Carolina. By this time, militia reinforcements had increased the American troops to about 1,100. Morgan decided to face Tarleton's force, and set up a defensive position at Cowpens, a place where militia often met to drill.

Morgan broke his men into three lines. The first line was sharpshooters. Behind them, he placed one group of militia. In the third position were Continentals and the Maryland and Delaware militia. A cavalry unit was held in reserve.

Tarleton arrived at about 7:00 A.M. on January 17, and immediately attacked. The American sharpshooters quickly blasted the British horsemen and forced them back. Tarleton's forces charged again, with their swords drawn, but the reserve American cavalry unit met them and forced a second British withdrawal. Before long, the British broke ranks and fled. Tarleton tried to rally his troops, but they refused to fight any longer.

The Battle of Cowpens was one of the great American victories of the Revolution. Within 50 minutes, 300 British were killed and wounded. More than 700 British soldiers were taken prisoner. The British also lost 800 muskets, 2 cannons, 100 horses, and 35 supply wagons. Only 12 Americans were killed and 60 wounded in the battle.

Though Morgan had won the battle at Cowpens, he was far from safe. Cornwallis's army was still between Morgan's men and the American army under Greene—and Cornwallis was so upset about the defeat at Cowpens that he turned immediately north to destroy Morgan, and, eventually, to take on Greene.

After Cowpens, Morgan withdrew northward. January was a rainy month, yet Cornwallis moved constantly in pursuit of Morgan's forces across North Carolina. Cornwallis wanted to catch Morgan so much that he burned his own supply wagons to be able to move more quickly. No matter how fast Cornwallis was, however, Morgan always stayed ahead of him, and met Greene who had returned from South Carolina to Gilbert Town, North Carolina, in early February.

In mid-February, the Americans arrived ahead of Cornwallis at the Dan River, just over the Virginia border. Cornwallis had hoped to catch Greene and force him into a battle, but Greene's army took boats across the river and left Cornwallis with no way to follow.

Cornwallis, disgusted, turned back to Hillsborough, at that time the capital of North Carolina. His men were tired and hungry, and Cornwallis needed to get supplies for them.

72

By March, Greene's army had increased to about 4,400 men. Because his forces now outnumbered Cornwallis's 2,000-man force, Greene was ready to fight. The American general had also selected the place and time for the battle.

The American army recrossed the Dan River and camped near Guilford Courthouse, North Carolina. While he waited for Cornwallis to attack, Greene established his men in positions that were similar to those of Morgan's troops at Cowpens. Behind a rail fence, he placed inexperienced North Carolina militia. From there, the militiamen could fire at the British, who had to cross the open fields. A little farther east, Greene placed the Virginia militia in thick woods. The British would not be able to charge easily through the forest. Another 500 yards away, he placed his regular Continental soldiers on top of a slight ridge behind a cleared field.

Cornwallis had waited for months for the opportunity to destroy Greene. Now Greene had challenged Cornwallis. On March 15, 1781, the British crossed Little Horsepen Creek and marched toward Guilford Courthouse. Most of the redcoats were tired by they time they arrived at the battle-field—they had marched 12 miles in a few short hours to get there.

As the British soldiers crossed the open field, more than 1,000 Americans fired their muskets from behind the rail fence. Dozens of British soldiers fell. The others moved forward and fired back. The inexperienced North Carolina militia,

73

surprised that the British continued the charge, ran from the battlefield.

Next, the British marched into the thick woods and came up against the Virginia militia. The British could not march in their usual formation because of the trees, so they split up into small groups. After 30 minutes of close fighting, the British broke through the American lines.

The British had already won two quick skirmishes, and now a third awaited them. One group of British infantry came out of the woods, charged across the field, and pushed toward the American regulars. The Americans held their ground, fired with discipline, and were able to force the British back into the woods.

On the other side of the field, a British battalion attacked the American left flank. The Americans were saved when a cavalry unit attacked the British from the rear.

Cornwallis was desperate for a victory, and, as he had while playing games at Eton, he would do anything to win. He ordered his artillery to fire into the group of British and Americans locked in hand-to-hand combat. Cannonballs killed as many British as Americans, but the fire prevented an American counterattack.

Charles Cornwallis

At Guilford Courthouse, Cornwallis ordered his artillery to fire on the battlefield while his own troops were in close combat with the Americans.

Greene, who saw the gap in the American line, feared a British breakthrough and ordered his men to retreat. He did not want to risk his whole army in this one battle.

The Americans left their artillery behind, because the horses that pulled the artillery wagons had been killed, and moved northward. Greene waited for a while to collect his men and then marched all night to a camp about 15 miles away. The Americans had suffered about 300 casualties out of the force of more than 4,000 men.

The British had suffered heavier casualties than the Americans. More than 500 British soldiers were dead or wounded—about one-fourth of Cornwallis's army. Cornwallis himself was slightly wounded, but refused to have his name put on the casualty list. Although the Americans had retreated, Cornwallis knew that the price of his victory was too high. "I never saw such fighting since God made me," he said. "The Americans fought like demons."

Though he had won the battle, Cornwallis could not pursue Greene because he had burned his supply wagons. There was little food to be found in the countryside, so the general ordered his exhausted and starving men to march eastward toward Wilmington, North Carolina. There, he expected to supply his men from cargo brought to the port by British supply ships sent north from Charleston.

Greene followed Cornwallis until April 8, then turned his army toward South Carolina, where he planned to attack supply depots and forts that supplied the British. Cornwallis did not pursue Greene because he thought that Loyalist forces in South Carolina and Georgia would stop Greene. Another reason that Cornwallis did not pursue

76

Greene was simply that he was closer to Virginia than he was to South Carolina. He had reached the conclusion that the British would be able to control the Carolinas only after Virginia had been conquered, which would prevent Patriot forces in the north from traveling through Virginia to the south.

Cornwallis's faith in the Loyalist forces in the south was misplaced. Greene's army fought Loyalist militia in the Battle of Hobkirk's Hill, which ended in a draw on April 25. Over the next few weeks, Americans captured six British forts, including Augusta, Georgia, on June 5. The British began to evacuate their forts in the interior of South Carolina. By August, they held only Charleston and Savannah, Georgia.

Throughout the spring, Cornwallis marched his army into Virginia. There, he joined forces with British troops under Benedict Arnold, the American who defected to the British side. Cornwallis knew that once he controlled Virginia, he could then invade the middle states by sending troop ships up the Chesapeake Bay.

Chapter 6

SURRENDER AT YORKTOWN

During much of the time Cornwallis was occupied in the Carolinas in 1781, Benedict Arnold had created chaos in Virginia. He led raids on warehouses and ports in which he destroyed huge amounts of the one cash crop the colonists had— tobacco. To try to stop Arnold, Washington sent 1,200 men to Virginia under the command of French ally Marquis de Lafayette (Marie Joseph Paul Yves Roch Gilbert du Mortier, Marquis de Lafayette).

OPPOSITE: Washington fired the first American artillery shot of the siege of Yorktown.

Lafayette became like a son to Washington during the Revolution.

Lafayette arrived in Virginia in March 1781, just as Clinton sent another 2,000 soldiers to assist Arnold. This group destroyed the Virginia militia outside Petersburg and raided the city. On April 29, Lafayette arrived at Richmond just in time to prevent the British from burning it to the ground.

In May 1781, Cornwallis arrived in Petersburg with 1,400 men. Shortly after, reinforcements joined him, which gave the British army about 7,000 soldiers. Cornwallis sent a message to Clinton to ask permission to carry on the war in Virginia as he saw fit, without concerns about events that took place farther south at Charleston or Savannah.

The Americans' main problem now became whether to fight a battle with Cornwallis's forces and be destroyed, or to avoid the enemy and carry out skirmishes that would do little damage to the redcoats. Lafayette decided to use the same hit-and-run tactics that had worked in the Carolinas, he retreated north to the Rapidan River in the eastern coastal region of the state. Cornwallis tried and failed to catch Lafayette, so he sent Tarleton's unit to raid Charlottesville, where the Virginia legislature was in session. During the raid, Tarleton came within minutes of capturing Governor Thomas Jefferson, who fled into the forest.

On June 10, General Anthony Wayne's brigade from Pennsylvania joined Lafayette's army in eastern Virginia. Then, a militia group of 600 riflemen also joined

After the Revolution, Anthony Wayne battled Native Americans in the Ohio River Valley.

Lafayette, which brought the American strength to about 5,000 men. Despite these added troops, the Americans could do little but shadow the British army and occasionally engage in skirmishes.

Meanwhile, in New England, events took place that soon affected Cornwallis. In May 1781, Washington and the commander of the recently arrived French forces, Lieutenant General Jean-Baptiste-Donatien de Vimeur, Count de Rochambeau, met in Wethersfield, Connecticut. Washington felt that their main objective should be

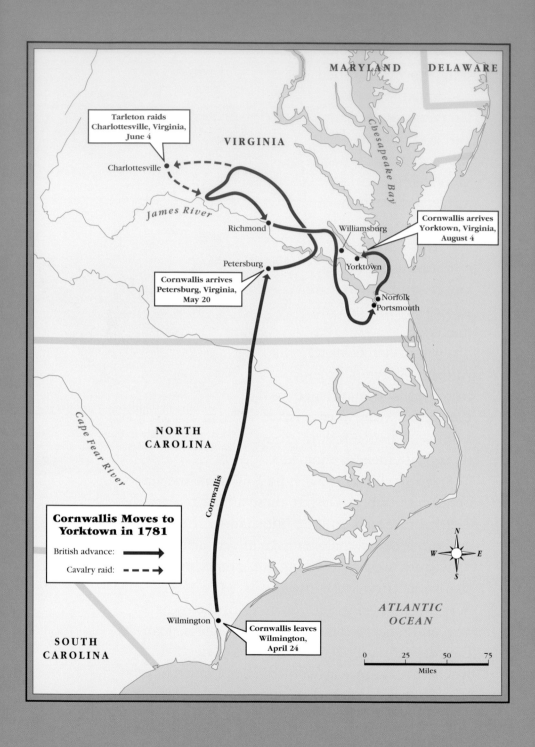

MARYLAND   DELAWARE

VIRGINIA

Tarleton raids
Charlottesville, Virginia,
June 4

Charlottesville

Chesapeake Bay

James River

Richmond

Williamsburg

Cornwallis arrives
Yorktown, Virginia,
August 4

Yorktown

Petersburg

Cornwallis arrives
Petersburg, Virginia,
May 20

Norfolk
Portsmouth

Cape Fear River

NORTH
CAROLINA

Cornwallis

**Cornwallis Moves to
Yorktown in 1781**

British advance: ⟶

Cavalry raid: ⤏

*ATLANTIC
OCEAN*

Wilmington

Cornwallis leaves
Wilmington,
April 24

SOUTH
CAROLINA

N
W   E
S

0   25   50   75
Miles

an attack on the British stronghold in New York City. Rochambeau, however, mentioned that it might be possible to send troops south to Virginia if favorable conditions arose there.

Favorable conditions soon did arise. In mid-June, a letter from Washington to Lafayette was intercepted by the British. In the letter, Washington revealed his plan to invade New York City. In response, Clinton, who had lived for a year in terrible, almost paralyzing, fear of a siege, immediately ordered Cornwallis to march east from his location near Richmond to a port area near Williamsburg. From there, he was to send half his force back to New York City by ship. Arnold was recalled to New York to aid in its defense.

Cornwallis, who had hoped to have the freedom to carry out a successful campaign in Virginia, once again found himself undermined by Clinton's orders. Not only had the size of his force been greatly diminished, the force that he did command was no longer able to continue its raids. Cornwallis's strong sense of duty would not allow him to question an order, but relations between the two men steadily worsened.

Clinton's order forced the large British force onto a narrow peninsula between the James and York Rivers. To march into such a vulnerable position did not concern Cornwallis because his force was several times larger than the American force. He was simply frustrated that he had to abandon his inland campaign.

Washington and Rochambeau believed that a siege would defeat British forces at Yorktown.

By mid-July, the combined French and American forces under Washington and Rochambeau had assembled north of Manhattan, but Washington had second thoughts about a direct attack on the British stronghold. His men had been easily stopped by the British in brief encounters at outposts over the previous weeks.

Clinton, too, had second thoughts about whether he needed reinforcements to his well-fortified position. The British had won several minor skirmishes on the outskirts of New York City. In late July, he canceled his order to Cornwallis. He ordered the southern commander instead to take control of a port area that was deep enough to allow both British warships and troop ships to dock. With New York secure, Clinton would send troops to begin a British campaign to control Virginia.

On August 1, Cornwallis occupied the port of Yorktown on the southern bank of the York River and village of Gloucester, across the water on the north bank. Again, Cornwallis was unconcerned about the fact that his troops were located in a poor defensive position. The Americans did not worry him.

Twelve miles away, in Williamsburg, Lafayette realized that under the right conditions, the American forces could actually defeat the mighty British army. In early August, Lafayette sent a messenger to Washington with the news of Cornwallis's move.

85

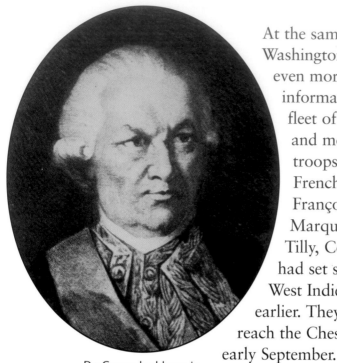

De Grasse had been in the French Navy for almost 40 years before the Revolution.

At the same time, Washington received even more encouraging information. A French fleet of 34 warships and more than 3,000 troops under the French admiral François Joseph Paul, Marquis de Grasse-Tilly, Comte de Grasse had set sail from the West Indies several weeks earlier. They expected to reach the Chesapeake Bay in early September.

On August 14, Washington made his decision. The French and American force, more than 8,000 men, would march as quickly as possible to engage Cornwallis at Yorktown. They broke camp on August 17, but left behind a small force stationed around New York City to create the impression that they still planned an attack there. This move fooled Clinton briefly and delayed his plans to send troops south.

The Americans and French marched 25 to 30 miles a day, and reached Philadelphia by September 1. There, they gathered supplies that had recently arrived from France on a transport ship captained by John Paul Jones, the famed

Charles Cornwallis

American naval commander who had fought off of England's coast for much of the war.

Although Cornwallis did not know it, his fate was about to be sealed. On August 30, De Grasse's French fleet dropped anchor in Chesapeake Bay. The French force, along with Lafayette's forces, could easily keep Cornwallis at Yorktown until Rochambeau and Washington arrived. The French admiral also offered Lafayette the services of his 1,800 sailors.

On September 5, de Grasse's fleet defeated a British fleet under Admiral Thomas Graves at the mouth of the Chesapeake Bay in an engagement known as the Battle of the Capes. As the allied armies headed south, the French navy blockaded the mouth of the York River, thereby forming a barrier between the river and the Chesapeake Bay. Cornwallis was trapped.

By this point, spies had informed Cornwallis that he faced a force of at least 8,000 enemy soldiers, while he commanded only about 3,000 men who were fit to fight, and another 2,000 slowed by disease. He came up with two possible plans to escape his situation. First, he could send a column of his soldiers down the road to Williamsburg and attack Lafayette's camp. His men would travel at night over the rough terrain to be ready for a dawn attack. Second, he could send an advance force of 2,500 men in small boats north up the York River to Queen's Creek, just above Williamsburg. These troops could attack at the rear of Williamsburg

In early September 1781, French ships destroyed the British warship *Sharon* and other British vessels in a battle on Chesapeake Bay.

while he and a larger group attacked the front of Williamsburg. After he considered both plans, Cornwallis decided to try the first plan.

Before he could put his plan into action, however, Cornwallis received a letter from Clinton that promised reinforcements. After he read the letter, Cornwallis decided to build defensive positions and wait for the reinforcements rather than risk possible defeat. Meanwhile, Clinton's

Charles Cornwallis

force sailed south, unaware that the mouth of the Chesapeake Bay was blockaded by the French.

On September 14, Rochambeau and Washington joined Lafayette at Williamsburg. Their armies were still hundreds of miles away—it would take 10 more days for all the soldiers to arrive. The French troops who had arrived by sea brought Lafayette's total forces to about 8,500 men. De Grasse also agreed to keep his ships in the Chesapeake Bay until the end of October.

At 5:00 A.M. on September 28, the French and American forces marched out of Williamsburg and set up camp south and east of Yorktown. Washington sent about 700 men across the York River to contain Cornwallis's troops at Gloucester. The American regulars around Yorktown numbered about 5,000. The militia added 3,000 more troops. The French had about 8,000 soldiers. Altogether, the French-American force outnumbered Cornwallis's army by at least two to one.

By late September, mosquitoes and unclean living conditions among the British at Yorktown had spread malaria, typhoid fever, and smallpox among the British troops. Cornwallis continued to cling to the hope that reinforcements would arrive from New York. When the news of the French blockade reached his headquarters, however, he had every available man dig defensive fortifications with renewed urgency. These workers included more than 2,000 African American slaves, who had fled to Yorktown after spies passed an offer throughout the region that promised slaves freedom if they aided the British.

The defenses the British constructed were essentially two curved lines of trenches for troops. These ditches—about four feet deep and seven feet wide—were interspersed with redoubts, raised earthen forts supported by logs, which served as artillery positions. Around the raised earthworks were barricades of sharp-edged branches called abatis.

The first line, called the inner defense, was about a mile-and-a-half long and was constructed closest to Yorktown. The outer defense line, farther from the town, partially blocked the main road from Williamsburg. This line had three well-armed redoubts built on its western and eastern ends, near the York River. They were called the Fusilier's Redoubt, Redoubt 9, and Redoubt 10.

On September 30, because he was short on men, Cornwallis abandoned his outer defenses. Washington quickly moved into these small fortifications on the outskirts of Yorktown. He had his men collect sticks and piles of dirt to use as protection while they dug trenches.

Cornwallis fired his cannons at these areas, with blasts every 20 minutes or so, and was able to kill and wound many Americans. When he discovered that he was running low on cannonballs, he tried to slow down the Americans by sending out patrols to attack the workers, which led to several bloody skirmishes.

Washington continued to have his men dig trenches and move cannons into them. By the morning of October 9, the 16-man gun crews were ready for action, and the trenches bristled with the muskets of French and American troops.

At 3:00 P.M. on October 9, the French artillery opened fire. American artillery began to fire two hours later. The cannons, which shot mainly 12- and 18-pound cannonballs and canister shot, fired around the clock. Even though the barrel would melt if a gun were fired more than once an hour, there were enough big guns to fire more than 1,700 shots a day—about 1 shot every 80 seconds—against the British.

The effect was devastating. When cannon fire hit, Cornwallis was forced to evacuate the home he had taken over for headquarters. He took cover in an earthen bunker behind the house. He soon found that the combined fire of several hundred French and American guns was much fiercer than the small numbers of American artillery he had encountered earlier in open battle. "The fire continued . . . until all our guns on the left were silenced . . . and our loss of men considerable," he wrote.

A British officer wrote that the bombardment was "one continual roar of cannon, mixed with the bursting of shells and rumbling of houses torn to pieces." A soldier wrote that he "saw men lying everywhere who were mortally wounded and whose heads, arms, and legs had been shot off."

★

In October 1781, Captain John Paul Jones was in Portsmouth, New Hampshire, prepared to take command of the new warship *America*.

★

91

On October 11, Washington ordered his force to move closer and construct a second parallel nearer to Yorktown, which would tighten their ring around the enemy. Work began, but enemy fire from Redoubts 9 and 10 on the eastern end of the British defenses drove the troops back. Allied artillery was unable to dislodge the British gunners and riflemen, and Washington was stopped.

Finally, after three days of exchanging fire, Washington ordered his troops to storm the redoubts. Each would be attacked by a force of 400 infantry men. The first task was to send men with axes to cut paths through the abatis. A storm of musket balls whizzed past the attackers as they cut through the barricades, but they were protected by fire from the allies and were finally able to complete the job.

After the paths were cleared, American soldiers led by Colonel Alexander Hamilton stormed Redoubt 10. French soldiers attempted to take Redoubt 9. The fighting was bloody, mostly hand to hand with swords and bayonets.

Eventually, at the cost of 25 allied soldiers, the British were forced off the redoubts. About 20 British soldiers were killed and more than 50 were taken prisoner. As soon as the redoubts were in allied control, they were linked to the second parallel, and artillery was positioned at even closer range.

On October 15, Cornwallis sent a message to Clinton. Cornwallis had been in enough battles to know that his situation was almost hopeless. "Our fresh earthen works do not resist their powerful artillery, so that we shall soon be exposed to an assault in ruined works...with weakened numbers," he wrote. "I cannot recommend that the fleet and army...risque [risk]...endeavoring to save us."

On the night of October 16, the desperate Cornwallis decided to lead his men in an escape. He planned to move his infantry across the York River to Gloucester under cover of darkness. There, against a lighter defense, he reasoned, the British troops might be able to break through and retreat northward toward New York. He left his sick and wounded—and his heavy guns—behind, and ordered more than 2,000 soldiers into a fleet of small wooden boats.

While the first wave of soldiers crossed the dark water, Cornwallis prepared to lead the second group across. Suddenly, a vicious rain and lightning storm began. In the driving wind and rain, two boatloads of soldiers were pushed helplessly down the York River, straight into the French navy. The escape plan was then canceled.

The men who made it across the river had little better luck. They returned to Yorktown on the morning of October 17, and told Cornwallis that the American defense was firmly entrenched. "Nothing passes in or out," reported one officer. Cornwallis knew then that his hours in command were numbered.

More than one-third of the British army in America surrendered with Cornwallis at Yorktown.

By this time, Washington had ordered his men to double the cannon fire. Cornwallis could not shoot back—he was out of artillery shells. About 10:00 A.M., he signaled surrender and sent a message to Washington. It read:

> *Sir:*
> *I propose a cessation of hostilities for twenty-four hours, and that two officers may be appointed by each side, to meet at Mr. Moore's house [Cornwallis's headquarters], to settle terms for the surrender of the posts at York and Gloucester.*

94

Negotiations between the two forces took place at the Moore House, which was half a mile behind British lines. Washington insisted that the British soldiers at Yorktown and Gloucester surrender and be confined as prisoners. He allowed the British officers to keep their weapons, and soldiers to keep their private property. Washington also demanded that the British march out of their fort with their flag furled, and that they play one of their own tunes. According to conventional eighteenth-century warfare, a surrendering army always played one of the enemy's tunes as a final gesture of defiance. To play their own tune would add a note of humiliation to the British surrender.

On October 19 at about 11:00 P.M., the signed surrender document was delivered to Washington. About noon, the French and American armies formed parallel lines as the surrendered British forces marched between them. The French wore bright blue coats. The Americans were dressed in tattered clothes. A few even had shoes.

Cornwallis did not lead his surrendering troops. He claimed illness and remained in his headquarters. Instead, the British were led by Brigadier General Charles O'Hara. As they marched, the British played a popular London tune called "The World Turned Upside Down."

Cornwallis's surrender ended all British attempts to control the 13 American colonies. He was allowed to leave for New York in November, and he returned to England in early 1782.

95

Sir Henry Clinton

Perhaps no other officer in the British army had as much of an effect on Cornwallis, and on the ultimate British defeat, as did Sir Henry Clinton. Clinton was born in Newfoundland, Canada, in 1738, where his father, Admiral George Clinton, served as royal governor. Clinton spent his early years in New York, where his father was governor from 1741 to 1751. Clinton's background resulted in a good start for his military career. He served in the Seven Years' War and rose quickly to the rank of colonel. In 1767, Clinton married Harriet Carter and, over the next five years, they had five children. In August 1772, Harriet Clinton died, which sent Clinton into a depression that left him unable to carry out any responsibilities or interact with friends and military colleagues for almost two years.

In 1775, Clinton was promoted to major general and ordered to America, where he fought with distinction at the Battle of Bunker Hill. By that time, Clinton had become unpopular with fellow officers and troops for his personality, which was a mixture of extreme shyness and insistence on having his own way. When Clinton became second-in-command to William Howe in 1776, his inability to interact with his superior and subordinates grew worse.

In 1777, Clinton was knighted by King George III, but the honor did little to gain him respect. Eventually, the extreme caution of his military strategy caused Clinton to conduct the war by avoiding defeat rather than gaining victory. His fear of defeat became so great that he attempted to resign from the British army several months before Yorktown.

When he returned to England after the Yorktown defeat, Clinton was widely blamed for the loss. His orders to Cornwallis had resulted in a reduction of Cornwallis's troops and his nearly indefensible position. While Cornwallis won honors in India and Ireland, Clinton wrote memoirs of the Revolution in which he laid the blame for the defeat on the British military and government. According to modern historian William Willcox, Clinton's book, *The American Rebellion*, was his explanation "for a career that failed. But the failure... came from a cause that he would have died rather than admit. His nemesis [worst enemy] was himself."

Clinton led British troops in the bloody battle of Bunker Hill in June 1775.

Postscript

Cornwallis's service in America was not the end of his career. In 1785, he became England's representative to the court of the Prussian emperor. The next year, he was made the viceroy, or governor-general, of the British colony of India. He spent seven years in India, during which he put down a rebellion of a sultan who opposed British domination. As a reward for actions in service to his country, King George III granted Cornwallis the title of marquis.

In 1798, Cornwallis was appointed viceroy and governor-general over Ireland. There, he helped put down an uprising by Catholic peasants and stopped French interference in Irish affairs. For three years, he was the major administrator in Ireland. Cornwallis worked hard to encourage Parliament to pass the Act of Union in 1800, a law that united the Irish and British parliaments, and resulted in further loss of freedoms for the majority of Irish people.

In 1802, Cornwallis became a British official in France. He was able to help arrange the Treaty of Amiens, which briefly ended the European conflict

Cornwallis continued to serve the Crown as a viceroy in India.

between Napoleon's France and England and the allies of each.

In 1805, he returned to serve as a viceroy in India. By this time, Cornwallis was 67 and in poor health. Not long after he arrived in India—on

October 5, 1805—he died of a fever near Ghazipore. In Cornwallis's honor, the British Empire built a huge mausoleum along the Ganges River in India to hold his remains, and also placed a statue of him in Westminster Abbey in London.

General Cornwallis—later Marquis Cornwallis—was a true patriot for his native country of England.

Cornwallis's service to England influenced historical events on three continents. Yet to most Americans, his name is remembered for just one short period in his life—the siege and surrender of Yorktown. Though many Americans might regard him as an enemy, throughout his life, he displayed a trait that is universally admired—a love of his country. Lord Charles Cornwallis was, to his own countrymen, a truly great patriot.

Charles Cornwallis

Glossary

artillery cannons, mortars, and other heavy guns used in the military

casualties during a battle, soldiers who are killed, wounded, or missing

commander a military leader, usually holding the rank of general

commission the appointment of an officer to a high rank in the armies and navies of the eighteenth century

ford a crossing of a stream or river

Hessian A mercenary soldier from Germany who fought for England during the American Revolution

Loyalist a person who lived in an American colony who remained loyal to the king of England during the American Revolution

militia citizens who armed themselves to fight against the British during an emergency, usually for a particular period of time

Parliament the legislative division of English government, made up of the House of Commons and the House of Lords

redcoats British soldiers who wore bright red field jackets

regiment a military unit smaller than a brigade and a division

reinforcements fresh soldiers sent to strengthen a military unit

siege the surrounding and blockading of a city, town, or fortress by an army in an attempt to capture it

skirmishes minor or preliminary conflicts or disputes

viceroy a person appointed by the king of England to head the government of one of the countries in the British Empire

For More Information

Books

Harmon, Daniel E. *Lord Cornwallis: British General.* Philadelphia, PA: Chelsea House Publishers, 2002.

Hibbert, Christopher. *Redcoats and Rebels: The War for America, 1770–1781.* London: Grafton, 1990.

Masoff, Joy. *American Revolution: 1700–1800.* New York: Scholastic, 2000.

Wickwire, Franklin and Mary. *Cornwallis: The American Adventure.* Boston: Houghton Mifflin Company, 1970.

Web Sites

Charles, Earl Cornwallis
http://jrshelby.com/kimocowp/cornwal.htm
Good biographical material from early years

Charles Cornwallis
http://famousamericans.net/charlescornwallis
Details on his contribution to the Revolution

Cornwallis, Charles
http://www.infoplease.com/ce6/people/AO813613.html
Basic biography with hyperlinks

Battle of Yorktown
http://www.patriotresource.com/battles/yorktown.html
An excellent all-purpose source for the Revolution with a time line and hyperlinks to biographies and battles

102

Index

104